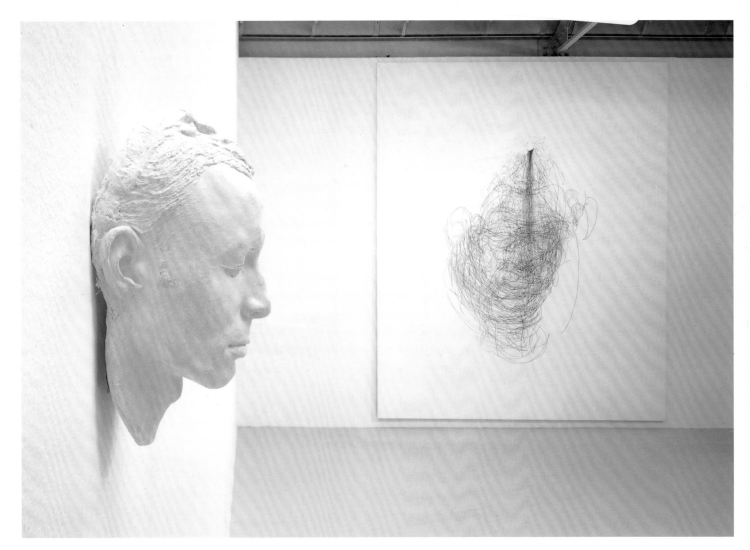

CLAUDE HEATH

Kettle's Yard and Christ's C

PREFACE

This exhibition marks the beginning of Claude Heath's residency in Cambridge as Kettle's Yard and Christ's College Artist Fellow.

Heath has rightly been recognised as one of the most interesting artists of his generation, bringing to his work a lively intelligence and a radical sense of enquiry. In addition to his appointment as the first artist-in-residence at The Henry Moore Institute in 1999, and a residency at Wimbledon School of Art in 2001, Heath has, since 1996, exhibited widely in Britain, and increasingly abroad. He has works in many private and public collections, including those of the British Museum, The Arts Council Collection, and the Walker Art Gallery, Liverpool.

The artist would like to express his particular thanks to Stuart Evans, Martin Holman, Tim Jefferies, Paul Kasmin and Clara Ha from the Paul Kasmin Gallery, Hales Gallery, Alex Templeton, Jo Wright, and all his family. We are especially grateful to Mel Gooding for his sensitive reading of Heath's work.

The Kettle's Yard Artist Fellowship is made possible by the continuing support of East England Arts and the hospitality of host colleges. The Master and Fellows of Christ's College continue to provide the Fellow with a studio for which we are veyy grateful.

Simon Groom, Exhibitions Organiser
Michael Harrison, Director

overleaf
Installation shot, 'Young British Artists VI', Saatchi Gallery 1996

SEEING THINGS

What do we see when we look at a Claude Heath drawing or painting? It's a harder question to answer than might appear at first sight. Harder in more ways than one. Because the difficulty is not simply that of defining what we mean by 'see', which is a matter problematic enough to have provoked the imaginative and scientific researches of countless philosophers, psychologists, artists and critics, and to exercise the mind of anyone thoughtful enough to recognise that there's more to most things than meets the eye. As time goes by, the very way we look at the world is subject to continuous modification, sometimes subtle and imperceptible, at certain moments drastic and surprising: we are constantly seeing things differently.

Thinking of Frank Stella's famous assertion about his own paintings, we might say: 'what you see is what you see', and begin by describing 'the visual facts'. (This is to avoid the ambiguity hidden in that laconically banal statement.) I'll try to simulate that kind of factual description later; I say, 'simulate', because when I attempt such a description of what I *see* I will be consciously eliminating from it a lot of things I *know*. We might attempt such a description (to ourselves, or for others) at our first encounter, but if we are at all interested (and you must be, or you wouldn't be reading this) we are going sooner or later to look at the drawing or painting again with more knowledge than we took to the experience in the first place. And then the 'facts' that we are aware of are going to be multiplied, and add to the complexity of the experience of 'seeing'.

It's not just that we might then know something about *how* Heath makes his drawings and paintings, and be intrigued by the implications of his methodologies. Writers on Heath have tended to concentrate on those aspects of the experience his work offers, and I am grateful to them for their observations and speculations. Heath's ways of working are indeed intriguing, and provoke thought about precisely the kinds of question I have been asking. An injunction from his artist father, one familiar to young art students, first stimulated Heath into thought about those questions: 'Don't draw what you know, draw what you see.' His – the young Heath's – predisposition to thinking about things was to be given full rein when he took a degree in philosophy; but he was aware from the moment that he began to draw that the teacher's simple instruction ignored not only the problem of what we mean by 'seeing' but also the problem of what we mean by 'knowing'.

Without taking it any further from the matter in hand – a drawing or a painting by Claude Heath – there are in the first case, of course, at least two people involved here in the business of seeing and knowing whatever it is they see and know: the artist and the viewer, and both, in the act of looking, are aware of the other. Let us begin with the artist. Drawing is a definitive human activity; it is a means to convey many kinds of information: the artist makes a drawing knowing that the activity has a long and complex history, not only in 'art'. Freed from certain conventions and expectations, the modern artist may claim that in the first place drawing might be a means to convey information to himself, a way to find something out; though it is difficult to say what. In this the modern draughtsman re-discovered the freedom of the child to use the process as a adjunct to learning about the world. Nevertheless, it is a two-way process: 'Drawing,' I once wrote, 'complicit with the act of looking, informs the eye's perception, reflects the world into the seeing mind; drawing, complicit with the act of thinking, informs the mind's conception, refracts the thought into the comprehending world.' The artist makes a drawing knowing it will be seen by others and thought about in a certain way, free of utility.

Knowing this to be the case, I wrote that in each generation 'artists take upon themselves the responsibility of re-learning the nature of drawing and developing its possibilities of expression. For artists whose impulses are experimental, for whom art is a kind of research, drawing becomes a mode of enquiry, a means to invention and discovery.' Claude Heath is just such an artist. But the artist's 'research' is not of the scientific or technical kind; the questions it asks, and the inventions and discoveries it comes up with, belong in the domain of the imagination; they have to do with our everyday reality, our thought and feeling as we move through space and time. Untrammelled by the baggage that comes with an Art School training, Heath simply became an artist by persevering in a perverse exercise, one often, as it happens, set for first year art students, which consisted precisely of *not* seeing what you draw (he wore a blindfold) and drawing from certain things he could get to know only from the sense of touch. More recently he has made drawings which do depend upon his sense of sight, drawing of things he can see made by the hand or hands unseen by his eye; in this mode we may say that it is his hands that are 'drawing blind'.

I deliberately refrained from saying that Heath drew what he 'felt', because the tactile is not something we can take any more for granted as a 'given' than the visual. As we all know, we cannot 'feel' without feeling. I mean 'feeling' here in the sense it has when we talk about 'thought and feeling', as denoting the affective. Touching is fraught with feeling. So much so that the idea of 'feeling' – affective response – has taken the word from the experience of the tactile. Just as, we may add, and very sharply to the point, the idea of knowing often takes words from the experience of the visual: 'I see', we say when the penny drops and we understand. 'Can't you see?' we demand of someone who is being obtuse. A person who knows things hidden from the ordinary eye is a 'seer', a 'visionary'. One of the things we seek from art is this kind of vision.

The artist translates what is, in a sense, invisible (that is, not yet seen in a certain aspect), and renders it actual and visible, as marks on paper, or on a wall. (In the case of many of Heath's drawings the object under scrutiny, so to speak, and which drawing will bring into a new visibility, is literally invisible to the draughtsman.) Mark-making is just what drawing is, and no small part of the excitement of drawing, for both draughtsman and spectator, is the magical reduction of visual experience to a physical object. (We may observe this excitement in children when they draw.) Objects in the world of three-dimensional space and light, having a certain colour and form, are reduced to the physical actuality of line and colour on the two-dimensional plane. Drawing is, then, a creative technology: by manipulation (handling) of a tool an object/image is created. New extensions of this technology – being extensions of a human function – create new possibilities of invention, new constructions, new kinds of information, new kinds of mediation and cultural exchange. Every drawing is a kind of proposition of what it is possible to know.

This is what makes Heath's drawings so exciting to the eye and to the mind. Here one recalls the American art historian Leo Steinberg's great formulation: 'the eye is part of the mind'.[1] Steinberg observed that every generation is faced by 'a new and unrepeatable facet of appearance.' The look of things changes. If the appearance of the world is thus 'unstable in the human eye' then its 'representation in art [is] not a matter of mechanical reproduction but of progressive revelation.' Steinberg's great essay is concerned to argue the persistence in art of the necessity of representation, linking that to the scientific ideas and 'metaphysical commitments' of its practitioners. It subsumes non-objective abstraction as the representation of energies, of 'trajectories and vectors, lines of tension and strain....' (Not, as it happens, a bad description of a Heath drawing, though Heath is of course pre-eminently a 'representational' artist.) 'Form in the sense of solid substance melts away and resolves itself into dynamic process.' It is not that the modern artist sets out 'to illustrate scientific concepts' so much as that 'an awareness of nature in its latest undisguise seems to be held in common by science and art.'

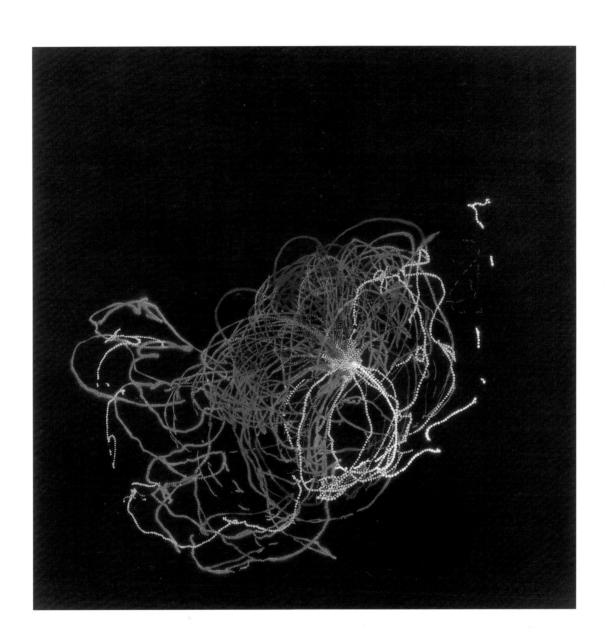

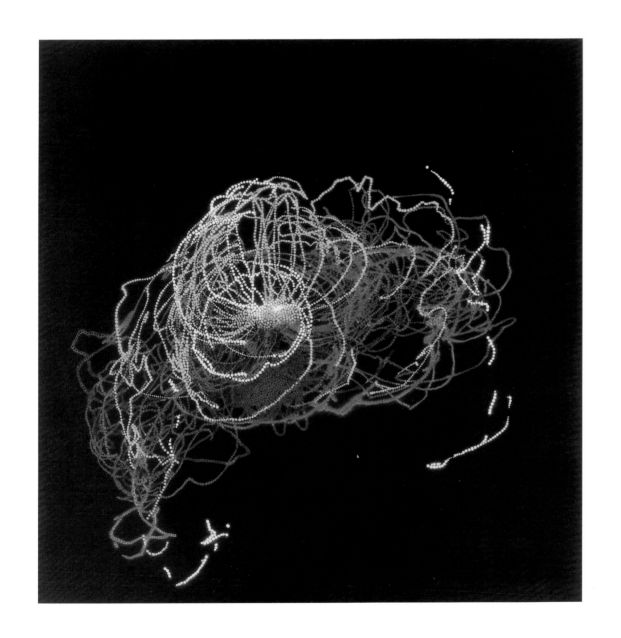 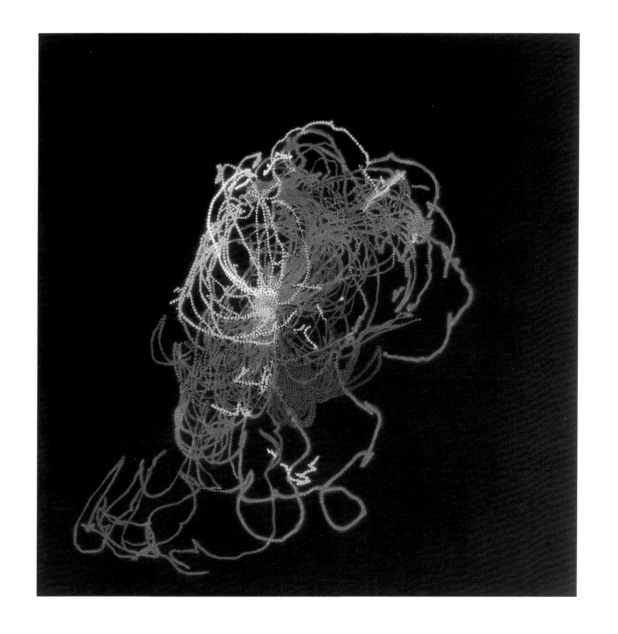

Let us turn to consider the experience of the viewer, and go back to the question with which I began this essay. We have established that what you see is compounded by what you know, and that it is difficult to define what we mean by either. Now, knowing by sight and knowing by touch are, in any case, quite different things, though both are means to that 'awareness of nature' which is the proper outcome of the work of art. The eye perceives colour and form as external to itself and to the body in which it is housed: sight is thus the purest and most objective of our senses. It provides the most direct information about time, and about space and the objects in it, intelligence untroubled by the physical ambiguities and sensory complexities in the responses of the body to touch. (We might add smell, taste and hearing, but we are here concerned with the visual and the tactile in art.) Touch, as U. Ebbecke, the German psychologist, described it, is 'bi-polar', having two components, seemingly indissoluble... one subjective with a body reference, the other objective, suggesting properties of objects.'[2]

I look at a painting by Claude Heath and what do I see? The space, or background, or the ground, or the space within which the pictorial action is taking place, is an all-over undifferentiated matt black. Set more or less centrally in the canvas rectangle there is a brilliant tangle of interweaving lines of electric colour. These are created of strings of coloured dots: white, yellow, red, blue, purple. The definition of the colours induces a re-consideration of the description of the lines as interweaving, for following each of the colour trajectories it becomes apparent (cognate with *to appear*) that these are, rather, *layered*, the one beneath, or by imaginative extension, behind, the other, in the order given. This suggests a temporal dimension, in addition to the spatial, in which the last named (purple) would have been the first laid down, with each colour closer to us being in effect closer to us in the time of its appearance. Even so, the first effect is of immediacy, and brilliance, as of a complicated firework, or a galaxy seen in colour; the darkness of the black suggesting the night sky. This is intensified by the chromatic intensity of the artificial colours: this nebula has a bright yellow concentration of dots at its centre. My response is one of delight, at the seeming contradiction between the complication of its creation and the spectacular immediacy of its visual effect (in fact just like the delight we take at an exploding firework): it is sight at work!

Already, of course, my description – to myself, to the reader – has been enlivened by imaginative comparisons, and the whole passage is textured by metaphor. Language will allow us no respite from that; discourse cannot proceed without the implicit metaphors that give words meaning. In fact I knew before I saw this painting that it was descriptive of – that it *represented* – something other than what I have described in my simulation'; and I knew also that it had been brought into being by certain

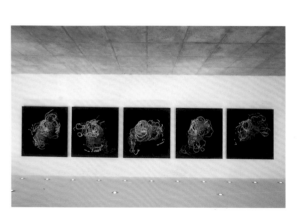

previous pages
'Pith 1', 1998, 'Pith 2', 1998, 'Pith 3', 1998,
all 119.5 x 114 cm, acrylic on linen. (Photos, FXP)

'Piths 1-5', 1998, installation shot, Hales Gallery, London. (Photo, FXP)

'Keeping the peel or 'Pith', attached to the base of the fruit, they were complex and rather unpredictable temporary structures liable to move and to break up. The aim was to make and draw these shapes simultaneously but by touch only, not looking at the orange itself, or the paper I was drawing on, and starting from a central core point. I was drawing them several times, covering the drawings afterwards and not looking at them, but turning the fruit around as it unpeeled and as I drew it. I used differing colours for different areas of the orange depending on how near or far they felt, and a piece of blu-tack as a fixed reference point on the paper to begin each line with. The smells and textures were a big part of the experience of drawing the orange, as well as being able to eat it afterwards.'

Claude Heath on the 'Peeling Oranges' series

procedures. In short, whatever it may 'look like', I knew that its origin was in touch, not sight, and that the painting itself was at a remove from the initial process, the original act of drawing in which the tactile found an equivalence in the visual.

The painting is entitled 'Peeling Oranges' and the image has its origins in the tactile sensations of that activity. The drawings from which it derives were made in pen on paper. The painting was made by mapping the drawings on to each other and projecting them by means of a stencil on to the canvas (hence the looping lines of overlapping coloured dots). The colours are arbitrary; they have no representational value, since touch has no colour; they have, however, a *descriptive* function, for they enable the viewer to see each separate action. In the final painted image the different times of the different actions, as registered in the drawings, are concatenated, and this is another aspect of the distancing that has occurred between the actions and the image that 'describes' them.

This 'distancing' is crucial to the project. Heath uses a number of devices whose purpose is to objectify, so to speak, the intensely subjective experience that is represented in graphic form in the final work. In addition to those already mentioned (choice of materials and support, choice of colours, stencilling, copying, over-lay of images) Heath uses left-hand and simultaneous double-handed drawing, projection, enlarging, juxtaposition of image surfaces, etc. These devices separate the viewer from the original act of the artist in his sensory encounter, by touch or sight, with the world. It is not to his purpose to give us any kind of access to his feeling (in either sense of that word) when we look at his drawings and paintings: it is the change effected in the viewer's way of seeing that counts, and the artist's own experience is simply not accessible to us. How could it be? For we cannot ever know what complex of thought and emotion, or what other senses accompanied the action, that were, to be more precise, part of the action. We can imagine for ourselves, drawing (!) upon our own experience, the stickiness, the smell, the strange sensual delight of peeling an orange.

As in all art, we are here confronted by more than meets the eye. For the peeling of oranges is itself a metaphor for tactile experience. The blindfold tracing of the outlines of a human face (that of a brother, or of a lover, say) is an act fraught with affective possibilities, with complex meaning, as is the tracing of the hand of a great sculptor, or the contours of a cast of the Willendorf Venus: art cannot give us the experience, it can give us a sign for it that might strike a chord in the responsive heart and mind. To do so it must distance itself from the turmoil of the haptic, come to meet us, as it were, as we approach it from the opposite direction, encountering it with the eye in another space than that in which the originating experience took place (wherever that was, whatever that was, however complex it may have been). It must free us to create our own response, to make the work work for us, in our space, the space (physical, mental, emotional) of our own experience.

In recent work, Heath has begun to investigate the experience of seeing itself. ('Investigate' is intended to connote research, but I bear in mind the differences between the work of science and the work of art). The objectivity that comes, uniquely among our senses, with the externality of the visual, is not without complications of its own, as we have seen. Seeing some things affects us deeply. But sight provides the artist with a distance from the subject to begin with. Heath has found ways of drawing that enable him to keep his distance from the object of his study, that deny him the familiar co-ordination of eye and hand that in drawing implicates the tactile in the visual. Descriptive drawing from the motif (such as Heath is making in these recent works) may be often an attempt to render the tactile impression that the object makes upon the eye: it reaches out to the object, so to speak, it *recognises* the form in space, its colour, its surface textures. As with the 'blindfold works', not only is the process of drawing reduced to registering what the sense delivers to the hand, but the procedures that follow, of superimposition, juxtaposition, etc. perform that essential function of objectifying the information, transforming it into a representative sign.

Heath's mapping on to the visual plane of tactile experience, or his transformation of the visual into pure touch (as in the recent drawings, where his eye cannot see the drawing), at once acknowledge subjective reality and eliminate subjective expression. His procedures are neither automatic, by means of which unpremeditated images are created by an abnegation of conscious control, nor those of what has been termed *écriture*, which is a personal sign-making, a subjective 'writing' of marks and figures whose emotive force is achieved by expressive idiosyncrasy. Nor is he concerned with finding a sign of the kind defined by Matisse, the apt and elegant reduction of the object to instant recognisablity and universality of application. His drawings and the paintings they generate are rooted in the actual. Whilst remaining in the domain of representation and extending the possibilities of objectivity they achieve, nevertheless, a rare distinction: seeking a new kind of intelligence, they have arrived at a new kind of beauty.

Mel Gooding

1. 'The Eye Is Part of the Mind', *Partisan Review*, Vol. XX, No. 2, reprinted in 'Reflections on Art',
   ed. Suzanne K. Langer, John Hopkins Press, New York, 1958.
2. U. Ebbecke, cited in 'Colour and Form' by Adrian Stokes, Faber & Faber, London, 1937.

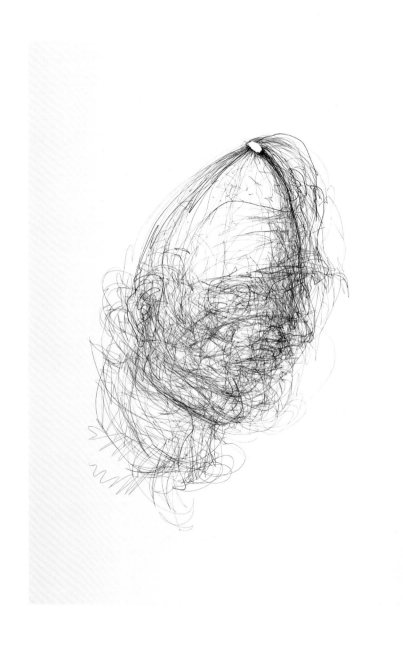

'Head Drawing' 1996.
75 x 50 cm, ink on paper.
Collection Henry Moore Institute, 1998. (Photo. Steve Marwood)

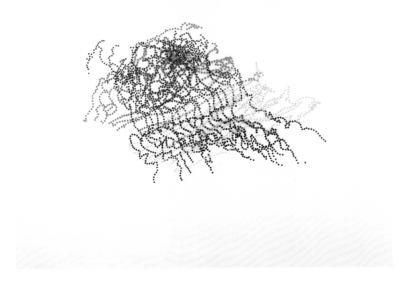

'Wave: Study for Wall Drawing' 1997.
 50 x 75 cm, acrylic on paper.
Collection Hugo Heath, London. (Photo. Steve Marwood)

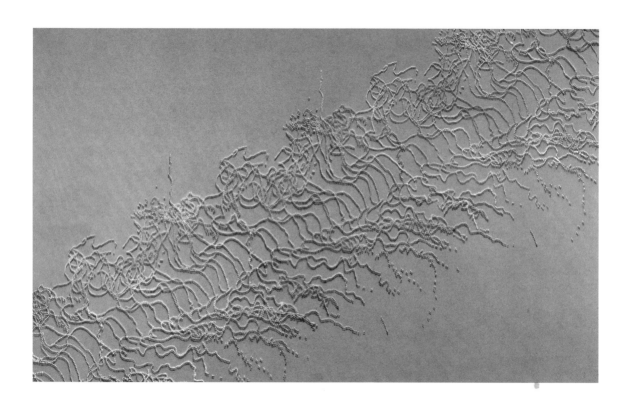

'Wave' 1997
acrylic on card.
Collection Stuart Evans, London.

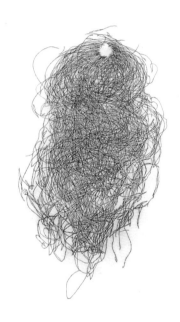

'Willendorf Venus' 1997.
150 x 339.5 cm, oil-based resin and chalk dust on canvas.
Collection Walker Art Gallery, National Museums and Galleries on Merseyside. (Photo. Walker Gallery)

Tiger and prey woodcarving, Bangladesh.

'Tiger and Prey' 1997.
213 x 427 cm, wall drawing. Installation 'Antechamber' Whitechapel Art Gallery, London.
(Photo. Whitechapel Gallery)

'Peeling Oranges' 1998.
30 x 42 cm, ink on isometric graph paper. *(Photo. FXP)*

'Peeling Oranges' 1998.
152 x 183 cm, acrylic on linen.
Collection Simmons and Simmons, London. (Photo. Steve Marwood)

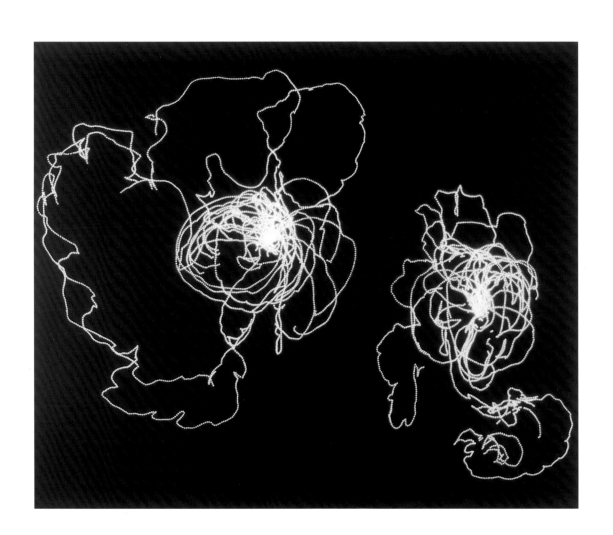

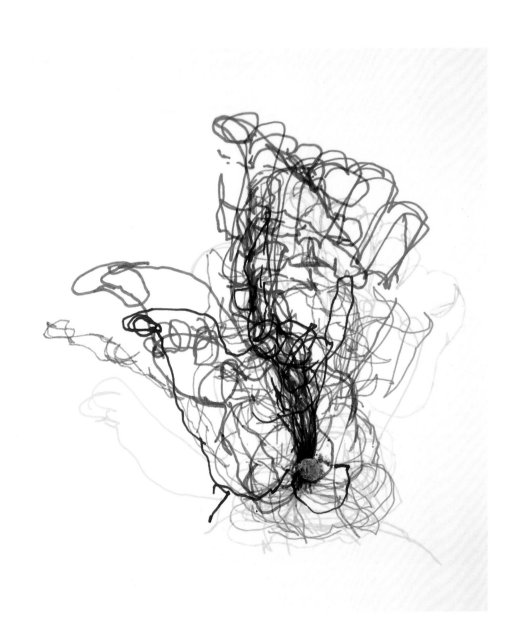

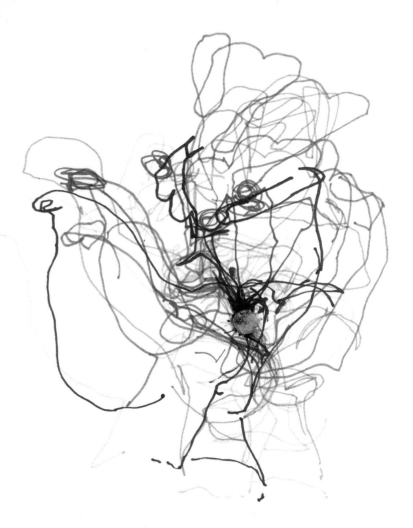

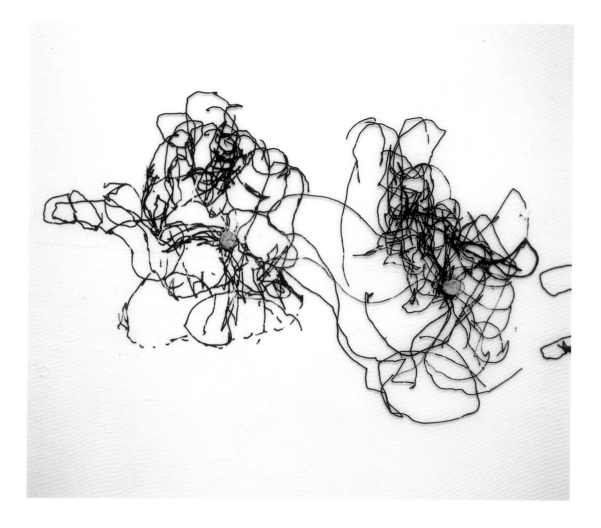

'Epstein's Hands' 1999.
114 x 148 cm, ink and Blu-tack on paper.
(details, overleaf)

'Epstein's Hand Rotating' 1999.
60 x 150 cm, ink and Blu-tack on Mylar. *(Photo. FXP)*
(detail, above)

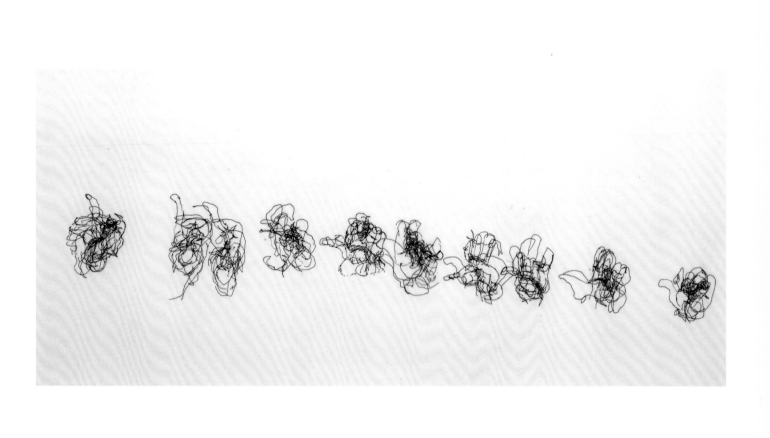

'A variety of means are used to transfer or enlarge drawings for the purposes of painting, including projection and digital means. Once scale has been decided upon, generally a template of some kind is made for the execution of the painting on whichever surface, or with whatever technique is being used, whether it is a linen or canvas prepared surface or a wall for a commissioned wall-drawing.

The template varies in material and specific purpose, and is sometimes used in conjunction with other templates. They are usually opaque and so the painting process is to a great extent hidden from sight during execution. The approach generally allows for a remaking of an image with a different emphasis, and to this end a variety of techniques are used.'

Claude Heath

'After Anthony Caro's 'Smiling Woman' 1956' 2000.
Wall drawing, dimensions variable. Installation 'Made Space' Pekao Gallery, Toronto.
(Photo. Fraser Stables)

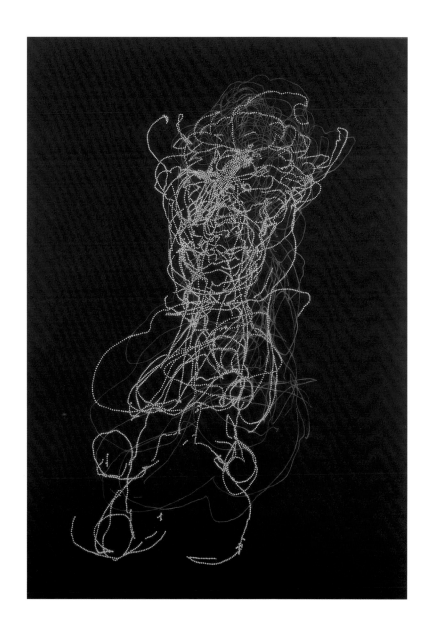

'After Anthony Caro's 'Smiling Woman' 1956' 1999.
280 x 200 cm, acrylic on linen.
(Photo.Walker Gallery)

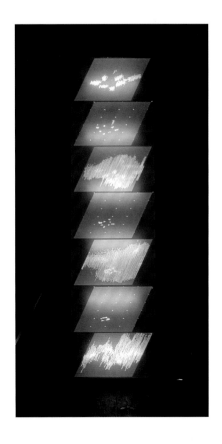

'The 'Fountain' lightboxes collectively form a single study of a fountain spray, presented from all four sides.

Seven drawings show descending heights within the fountain. Each drawing 'scans' the grid of a wire mesh as I gradually lowered it through the water spouts. The graduated marks are made one at a time on sheets of graph paper nearby, and covering them up as they accumulate in rows. (The parallel I find is with the game of 'Battleships', where what you have to go on is either "hit" or "miss".)

When the separate drawings are collated it is possible to see the three dimensional arrangement of rising and falling water. Water is something you can touch but it isn't especially dense to the fingers. It has a shape but a very complex and changing one, so it made sense to choose a definite but also very open-ended approach to drawing it in all its movement.'

Claude Heath

'Fountain' 2000.
Lightbox, 233 x 66 x 10 cm, greyscale Lambda duratrans print, aluminium lightbox.

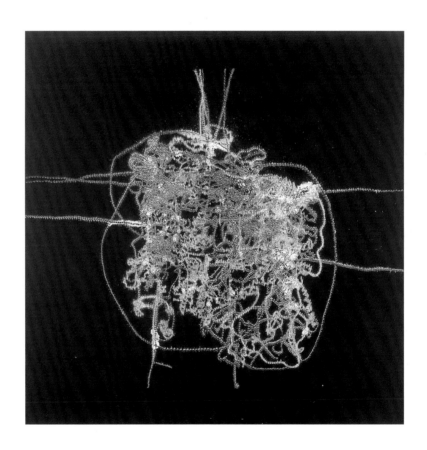

'Sedum burrito' 2002.
107 x 107 cm, acrylic on canvas
Collection Martin Holman, London. (Photo. Nick Manser)

'When you follow the movements of a football across a flat TV screen you sometimes have the sensation that the ball is going in a certain direction when it turns out to have a different arc altogether, and ends up at the feet of a different player than you had first thought. Its true movements are hidden by the flatness of the screen until it arrives at some particular part of the pitch. This same kind of sensation sometimes happens while drawing, when you attempt to compress the sight and touch of a solid object onto various parts of a flat surface.

It seems that one solution to the problem that I had set myself was to develop the drawing equivalent of a split screen format, which allows one to see the relative positions of objects. The slides show how the drawings began to incorporate the various angles of approach, through the folding of the paper to encompass different aspects of an object.'

Claude Heath

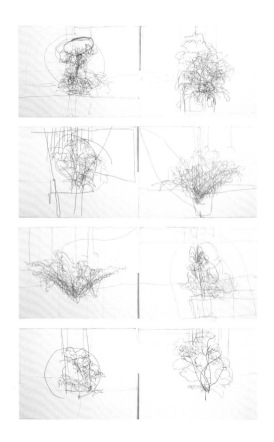
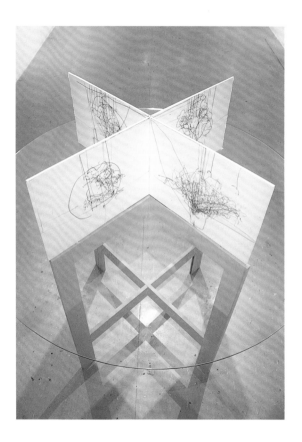

'Four-Fold Drawing / Four Plants' 2001.
Two parts, each 84.5 x 29.5 cm, acrylic ink on paper, mounted on 5mm board.
Installation Wimbledon School of Art, Centre for Drawing. *(Photo Nick Manser)*

CLAUDE HEATH

Born 1964 London.
Lives and works in London.
B.A. Philosophy, 1983-1986,
King's College, London.

Solo Exhibitions

2001 'Claude Heath' The Centre for Drawing at
Wimbledon College of Art, London.
'Claude Heath' Paul Kasmin Gallery, New York.

2000 'Art In Sacred Spaces' Christchurch, Isle of Dogs,
London, with other venues.

1999 'Claude Heath Drawing from Sculpture' The Henry
Moore Institute / Leeds City Art Gallery.

1998 'The Pith and the Marrow' Hales Gallery, London.

1995 'Claude Heath' Hales Gallery, London.

Group Exhibitions

2002 'Mapping The Process' Essor Gallery, London.
'Prospects 2002' Pizza Express Drawing Prize
Exhibition, Essor Gallery Project Space, London.
'Head On: Art with the Brain In Mind' Science
Museum, London.

2001 'Sages, Scientists, and Madmen' One In The Other,
London.
'The Jerwood Drawing Prize 2001' Cheltenham &
Gloucester College/ London/ Geneva.
'Fall Show' G Fine Art, Washington.
'Summer 2001' Paul Kasmin Gallery, New York.
'Paper Assets: Collecting Prints and Drawings
1996-2001' The British Museum, London.
'Systems: Past-Present-Future' TIAA/CREF, New York.

2000 'Made Space' touring exhibition; Pekao Gallery,
Toronto, Canada; The Changing Room, Stirling,
Scotland; The Talbot Rice Gallery, Edinburgh,
Scotland.

1999 'Recent Acquisitions, Leeds Sculpture Collections'
The Study Galleries, Leeds City Art Gallery.
'Fresh Paint: Works from the Frank Cohen
Collection' Glasgow Museum of Modern Art,
Scotland.
'Drawings' Nicole Klagsbrun Gallery, New York.
'Claude Heath, Leo De Goede, DJ Simpson,
Alexis Harding, Andrew Bick' Gallerie Hollenbach,
Stuttgart.
'The NatWest Art Prize' Lothbury Gallery, London.
'The John Moores Exhibition 21' Walker Art Gallery,
Liverpool.

1998 'Works on Paper' Duncan Cargill Gallery, London.
'The Jerwood Painting Prize' The Jerwood Gallery,
London.
'From Within / D'all Interno' Juliet Gallery, Trieste,
Italy.
'The Whitechapel Open' Whitechapel Gallery,
London.
'Le Doux Dessin' Hasselt, Belgium.

1997 Prizewinner, 'The John Moores Exhibition 20'
Walker Art Gallery, Liverpool.
'Klarsehend' One In The Other, London.
'Low Maintainance / High Precision' 172 Deptford
High Street & Hales Gallery, London.
'Blueprint' De Appel Foundation, Amsterdam.
'Antechamber' Whitechapel Art Gallery, London.

1996 'Young British Artists VI' The Saatchi Gallery,
London.
'The Whitechapel Open' Whitechapel Gallery,
London.

1995 'To Whom It May Concern' Anna Bornholt Gallery,
London.

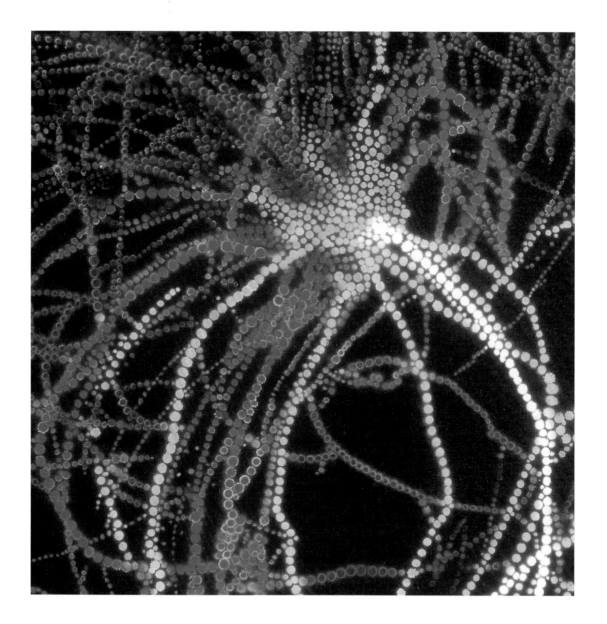

'Pith 1' 1998. (*detail*)

Kettle's Yard, University of Cambridge, 28 September - 3 November 2002

catalogue designed by Paul Allitt
printed by Hilo Colour Printers Ltd, Colchester
© Kettle's Yard and Claude Heath 2002

ISBN 0 907074 96 0

This and other Kettle's Yard publications are available from
Kettle's Yard, Castle Street, Cambridge, CB3 0AQ
telephone 01223 352124 • www.kettlesyard.cam.ac.uk